# Six Spiritual Needs In America Today

## Sermons With Chancel Dramas

### Arley K. Fadness

CSS Publishing Company, Inc., Lima, Ohio

SIX SPIRITUAL NEEDS IN AMERICA TODAY

Copyright © 1997 by
CSS Publishing Company, Inc.
Lima, Ohio

Original purchaser may photocopy the chancel dramas for use as intended. All other rights reserved. No other part of this publication may be reproduced in any manner whatsoever without the prior permission of the publisher, except in the case of brief quotations embodied in critical articles and reviews. Inquiries should be addressed to: Permissions, CSS Publishing Company, Inc., P.O. Box 4503, Lima, Ohio 45802-4503.

Scripture quotations are from the *New Revised Standard Version of the Bible*, copyright 1989 by the Division of Christian Education of the National Council of the Churches of Christ in the USA. Used by permission.

**Library of Congress Cataloging-in-Publication Data**

Fadness, Arley K., 1937-
   Six spiritual needs in America today : sermons with chancel dramas / Arley K. Fadness.
     p.  cm.
   ISBN 0-7880-1151-0 (pbk.)
   1. Christian life—Sermons. 2. Self-actualization—Religious aspects—Christianity. 3. Sermons, American. I. Title.
BV4501.2.F     1998
252—dc21                                                            97-36686
                                                                                                  CIP

This book is available in the following formats, listed by ISBN:
   0-7880-1151-0   Book
   0-7880-1152-9   IBM 3 1/2
   0-7880-1153-7   MAC
   0-7880-1154-5   Sermon Prep

PRINTED IN U.S.A.

*To Pamela,
my wife and encourager,*

*and to my four children,
Timothy,
Susan,
Joel,
and Rebekah*

# Table Of Contents

**Preface** — 7

**1. The Need To Believe That Life Is Meaningful And Has Purpose** — 9
Worship Aid
Drama: *Crossing The Desert (Of Life) And Findin' Nuttin' But Sand, Sun, And Superficiality*
Sermon: *What Are You Holding On To?*

**2. The Need For A Sense Of Community And Deeper Relationships** — 21
Worship Aid
Drama: *I Just Need To Talk To A Real Person*
Sermon: *No Longer Home Alone*

**3. The Need To Be Appreciated And Respected** — 33
Worship Aid
Drama: *The Conference*
Sermon: *You Are My Beloved*

**4. The Need To Be Listened To And Heard** — 47
Worship Aid
Drama: *Can Anybody Really Hear Me?*
Sermon: *Is Anybody Listening?*

**5. The Need To Feel That One Is Growing In Faith** — 61
Worship Aid
Drama: *Same Old, Same Old*
Sermon: *Growing In God's Freedom*

**6. The Need For Practical Help In Developing
   A Mature Faith**     73
Worship Aid
Drama: *The Dilemma*
Sermon: *Surrounded By Help*

# Preface

I was stunned and graciously affirmed by the positive response from my congregation, Messiah Lutheran of North Mankato, to the *Six Spiritual Needs In America Today* sermon series. The six needs, as identified by a George Gallup, Jr., poll in the '90s, are obviously rooted deeply in the human psyche and call for renewed attention.

Praise, Alleluias, and Antiphons to the preacher, teacher, counselor who blesses congregational life with pastoral insight and relevant proclamation.

The dramas, played and critiqued by the Messiah Players Drama Team, Diane Halverson, Merry Stewart, Ron Polzin, Audrey Schlong, Cindy Flitter, and Lois Smook, are intended to be used to prepare the hearers for the proclamation of the Good News.

Arley K. Fadness

# 1

## *Worship Aid*

A Chancel Drama suggestion for the sermon, "What Are You Holding On To?" is titled "Crossing The Desert (Of Life) And Findin' Nuttin' But Sand, Sun, And Superficiality." It is an original drama by Arley K. Fadness.

**Synopsis:** A traveler crossing the desert (of life) seeks a cool drink that will really satisfy. A bartender offers drinks that are only temporary. The traveler meets other travelers who are thirsty as well. All conclude they are thirsty for something more lasting than what the bartender has to offer.

This chancel drama is a setup for preaching to the theme of "The Need To Believe That Life Has Meaning And Purpose."

# Crossing The Desert (Of Life) And Findin' Nuttin' But Sand, Sun, And Superficiality

**Text:** Luke 18:18-30

**Theme:** The Need To Believe That Life Has Meaning And Purpose

**Characters:** Travis (a travelin' man)
Bartender Joe
Olympic Athlete Chad
Sad Selma, college dropout
Clancy Clown, dressed as a clown

**Tone:** Mix of humorous and serious

**Setting/Props:** The Last Chance Bar

**Approximate time:** 5-6 minutes

---

(Music: Sons of the Pioneers' "Cool, Cool Water" or some current "water" song)

**Travis:** *(Appears on stage, crawling on the floor)* Water, water, bottled, Artesian, mineral, anything wet!

**Bartender:** How about this Handy Wipe? Heh, heh. Just kiddin', podner. What'll you have?

**Travis:** *(Groans)* I'm dying.

**Bartender:** Mortuary's across the street.

**Travis:** *(Starts rising, leans on bar)* Hey — I've been crossing this here desert fer three days now. Canteen went dry yesterday. 108 in the shade.

**Bartender:** *(Leaning on bar)* Yeah, it's hot out there.

**Travis:** *(Feels bartender's face)* Sure you're not one of them mirages?

**Bartender:** *(Laughs)* Well, I might be and I might not be. What'll you have?

**Travis:** Whatiyah got?

**Bartender:** Depends on your taste. Yah really thirsty?

**Travis:** Could drink the Mississippi dry today.

**Bartender:** You crossed the Mahara Desert you say?

**Travis:** Yep.

**Bartender:** By foot?

**Travis:** Naw.

**Bartender:** Mule? Horseback?

**Travis:** *(Mysteriously)* Neither.

**Bartender:** You gotta Jeep out there? *(Points outside)*

**Travis:** Yep.

**Bartender:** Really!

**Travis:** It's mine.

**Bartender:** Came in that? And you're thirsty?

**Travis:** Yep. Now whatchya got to drink?

**Bartender:** *(Still talking about the Jeep)* Air conditioned?

**Travis:** Yep. What's in that jug? *(Points)*

**Bartender:** *(Puzzled)* Don't see any sand on it. None on yer clothes.

**Travis:** Jeep's airtight. Four-wheel drive. Cell phone. Passenger TV. Got it all.

**Bartender:** Whoa — you got all that and still you're thirsty??? You got to be kiddin'.

**Travis:** *(Angrily)* Hey, dude. Is this the Last Chance Bar or what? Ya got drinks, ain't yah?

**Bartender:** *(Regains composure)* Well, yes — and your trip across the Mahara Desert hasn't taken you three days, has it? *(Pause)* How old are you, friend?

**Travis:** Thirty. *(Irritated)* What's that got to do with gourds in Greece?

**Bartender:** Your desert travels have really taken you **thirty years**! Not three days.

**Travis:** Well — yeah. If you put it that way. I'm bummed!

**Bartender:** Okay. I see.

**Travis:** See what?

**Bartender:** Here's *(show bottle)* what might help. Tranquility for the Trail. Improves your self-worth. Only temporary though.

**Travis:** Naw. What else yah got?

**Bartender:** Well, here's a blend of Hopps and Barley. Called Ego Booster.

**Travis:** I'm really thirsty — could use a shot of that.

**Bartender:** *(Shows another jug)* Gin and Grin. Great upper.

**Travis:** *(Pushes sample drinks aside)* Naw, I need a **real** drink! Something, something —

**Bartender:** Yes?

**Travis:** Something that satisfies not just here but here. *(Points to stomach and then heart)* Something deep.

**Bartender:** You mean spiritual? I'm not a priest — *(brightly)* but **I do** priestly things.

**Travis:** Like?

**Bartender:** Like listen to confessions, give advice, counsel ...

**Travis:** Oh, yeah? Give me something that really lasts, will yah? What's with him? *(Points to athletic-type person who is very morose and has been sitting at the bar.)*

**Bartender:** He just came in before you. Said he's thirsty, too.

**Travis:** Hey, how ya doin'?

**Chad:** Who, me?

**Travis:** Yeah. Been in the desert?

**Chad:** Yep. Just came back from the Olympic Games in Atlanta.

**Travis:** How'd you do?

**Chad:** Won a medal. 200 meter dash. Worked for ten years for that goal. *(Brightens up)* Wow! Was that something great! *(Gets excited; jumps up)* I ran. I ran with everything I got ... ooo ...

**Bartender:** I saw you on TV. Great run. Let's see your medal. Quite a thrill, eh?

**Chad:** *(Glumly)* You know it **was** then. It was great ... but ...

**Travis:** But what?

**Chad:** Now what? For years I dieted, trained, disciplined, worked out, ran hard, achieved my goal ... but now what?

**Bartender:** *(To Travis)* I think he's actually depressed.

**Travis:** You're right — Father — *(laughs)* ... What about her? *(Points to a sad Selma)*

**Bartender:** Dunno. Comes in every day from the desert. Orders a Gin and Grin. Says she's a college dropout. No major. Not even a minor. She says she's not sure where she's going. Kinda confused. Generation X, you know.

**Travis:** What about him? *(Spotlight on clown who has been in the shadows till now)*

**Bartender:** Ask him.

**Travis:** Hey, I'm Travis. Just came off the desert. How are you doing, man?

**Clown:** Clancy Clown's my name.

**Travis:** What do you do?

**Clown:** Make people laugh and laugh and laugh and laugh. *(Fakes laugh; goes into a routine)* You know why cannibals don't eat clowns, don't cha? *(Pause)* Cause they taste funny. Ha Ha. *(After a few antics goes and sits sadly at the bar.)*

**Bartender:** And what makes **you** laugh?

**Clown:** Nobody. *(Long pause)* Just give me one of them ... *(points to a jug)*

**Travis:** *(To bartender)* You've got a good business here, Joe.

**Bartender:** Unfortunately, yes.

**Travis:** Unfortunately?

**Bartender:** Yes, unfortunately. I'd rather do something else. Sure I'm kinda priestly for some, but I'd rather you folks got a drink that lasted, that filled you deep and quenched your true thirst. Something that kept you healthy and fulfilled and focused ...

**Travis:** Yeah — I know what you mean!

(Music)

The End

# *What Are You Holding On To?*
## Luke 18:18-30

*"A certain ruler asked him (Jesus), 'Good teacher, what must I do to inherit eternal life?' Jesus said ..."*

Brothers and Sisters in Christ,

I am pleased to announce a Preaching Series based on a recent poll on the spiritual needs of Americans. According to George Gallup, Jr., six spiritual needs surfaced in that nationwide poll. They are:

1) The need to believe life is meaningful and has a purpose.
2) The need for a sense of community and deeper relationships.
3) The need to be appreciated and respected.
4) The need to be listened to and to be heard.
5) The need to feel that one is growing in faith.
6) The need for practical help in developing a mature faith.[1]

This morning we consider the number one need of **believing life is meaningful and has a purpose.** Seventy percent of those polled cited this need. Let me begin with a marvelous story Michael Foss tells. It's about an executive in a high-rise office building in New York City.

The executive had a seven-foot fluorescent light that had burned out. But in the office building only the janitors could replace light bulbs, and the cost was twenty dollars. In his mind this was exorbitant. So he decided he would replace it himself. He went to a lighting outlet near his home and bought the proper light bulb and got up early the next day, drove his car into town, caught the subway into the city, carrying the seven-foot fluorescent bulb all the way, and sneaked in through the foyer before anyone else was there except the security guard. Then he replaced the bulb. He took the old tube and placed it up against the wall behind his desk chair so no one would see it. And for the rest of the day he pondered how he would get the burned-out bulb past the janitors. Finally he had an idea. He had seen a construction site near where he had boarded the subway, so he would stay late, sneak out of the building carrying the burned-out tube and toting it on the subway, and get off at his stop. But instead of going to his car, he would take the tube to that construction site and put it in their dumpster.

So he called his wife and told her he would be working late. He waited until well after six o'clock and successfully sneaked through the lobby, and, holding the fluorescent tube vertically, sat down on the subway.

And that's when events overtook him. An amazing thing began to happen. As the subway began to fill up, more and more people came and held on to that fluorescent light as if it were a stanchion. Finally, when he reached his destination there were six people hanging on to his light tube and he had a better idea. When his stop arrived, he simply got up and walked out ... leaving those six people holding onto his fluorescent light as if it were a stanchion.[2]

Beloved People of God, the number one question this morning is: What Are You Holding On To? What gives your life meaning and purpose?

A certain young man, a rich young ruler, came to Jesus and asked, "Teacher, what must I do to inherit eternal life?" Another way to ask it is: "How do I find meaning and purpose in **life** and in the **life to come**?"

This rich young ruler, no doubt, was a good person. But there gnawed at him a restlessness and a feeling that something was lacking within his heart and soul.

He was searching for something to fill the void. He needed something to hang on to.

Dr. Victor Frankl, a concentration camp survivor and a psychotherapist, wrote a wonderful book titled *Man's Search For Meaning*. The book is now in its seventy-third printing. It has been published in twenty languages, and the English editions alone have sold over 2.5 million copies.

When asked about the success of his book, Frankl replied, "I do not at all see in the best-seller status of my book so much an achievement and accomplishment on my part, as an expression of the **misery** of our time; if hundreds of thousands of people reach out for a book whose very title promises to deal with the question of meaning in life, it must burn under their fingernails."[3]

Come back to the New York executive. I wonder what happened at the end of the line? I picture a man or woman suddenly discovering that he or she is left holding a burned-out fluorescent light tube and not a subway stanchion after all, and I wonder what he or she did with it.

Or, a more unpleasant scenario might be that the subway car came to a sudden stop and those who were holding the burned-out tube dramatically discovered that what they thought was a source of security and stability was neither. What a mess!

What are you holding on to? You want your life to be filled with meaning and purpose. Can we find it by trying to obey the **Law**?

The young ruler did not murder. He did not commit adultery. He honored his father and mother. He obeyed the commandments, at least this is what he told Jesus. But the **Law** never brings happiness. It brings either **pride** or **despair**.

What are you holding on to? Your **wealth**? The young ruler was rich. But he couldn't give it up. "His countenance fell," says the Bible. He went away sad and discouraged.

Is there meaning in what you buy and sell and create and invent? You've seen the sign, "I Shop Till I Drop." Or that bumper sticker, "This Car Stops At All Garage Sales." What are you holding on to?

Will **success** do it? It didn't for Buzz Aldrin. Remember Buzz Aldrin? Over two decades ago we listened intently to the radio as first Neil Armstrong and then Buzz Aldrin set foot on the moon. These two men quickly became household names. Their accomplishment was legend.

Even though two decades have passed since their moonwalks, you still might recall Aldrin and Armstrong's years of hard work, dedication, and discipline that prepared them to walk on the moon. What you might not recall, however, was Aldrin's later emotional breakdown and his slow, painful recovery.

Buzz Aldrin said it resulted from the terrible disillusionment he felt after working so hard, achieving every goal set before him, and then finding it all empty when it was over. His dreams, fantastic though they were, were not lasting enough. He walked on the moon, but after that — no purpose, no meaning.

Nowadays there's a great search for meaning in **self**. I read somewhere that just before Franklin Delano Roosevelt was inaugurated as president, someone made an attempt to assassinate him. After the would-be assassin was captured, the authorities grilled him. "Are you a member of the Ku Klux Klan?" "No." "Are you a member of a radical union?" "No." Finally they asked him, "Do you belong to a church?" He responded by saying, "No, I belong only to myself ... and I suffer."

Where then does meaning come from? Take a look at Psalm 8 and David. David, the greatest king that ever lived in Israel's history and life, found himself searching. Some believe David wrote Psalm 8 after a great victory in his life. Chuck Swindoll suggests that this song was composed by David after he killed the giant Goliath.

If so, picture David, like Buzz Aldrin. He is a great hero in his country. He has earned the praise of people everywhere, but something is not right. As he prepares to go to bed that night he can't sleep. He feels empty. He wanders outside. He looks up into the Milky Way and he asks the questions you and I ask in moments of quiet and reflection: "Who am I? What is humankind? Why am I here? What is my purpose in life?" In David's words,

> *When I look at your heavens,*
> *the work of your fingers,*
> *the moon and the stars that*
> *you have established;*
> *what are human beings that you*
> *are mindful of them,*
> *mortals that you care for them?*

David doesn't stay depressed as long as did Buzz Aldrin. Immediately he answers his own question:

*Yet you have made them a little
lower than God,
and crowned them with glory
and honor.
You have given them dominion
over the works of your hands;
you have put all things under their feet.*
— Psalm 8

And as David pondered the answer, especially his place in the eternal scheme of things, life took on meaning and purpose for him."[4]

What are you holding on to?

I'm holding on to Christ. And as I hold on to Christ I realize God has held on to me long before through God's amazing grace and wondrous mercy.

Let go of anything that offers nothing but empty promises and broken words. With Christ I live — and my life has meaning and purpose. Amen.

---

1. George Gallup, Jr., *National & Religion Report*, Volume V, Number 11 (May 20, 1991), p. 1.

2. Michael Foss, Easter Sermon, 1993, Prince of Peace Lutheran, Burnsville, Minnesota.

3. *Faith at Work*, Volume 106, No. 1, Jan/Feb 1993, p. 3., Faith at Work Inc., 150 South Washington Street, Suite 204, Falls Church, Virginia 22046.

4. *Ibid., FAW*, p. 3.

# 2

## *Worship Aid*

A Chancel Drama suggestion for the sermon, "No Longer Home Alone," is titled "I Just Need To Talk To A Real Person." It is an original drama by Arley K. Fadness.

**Synopsis:** Hattie, an elderly woman who is homebound, attempts to make contact with the outside world through her latest technological wonder — a cell phone. She encounters the same difficulties with voice mail that most everyone has experienced. Hattie longs for human contact.

This chancel drama is a setup for preaching to the theme of "The Need For A Sense Of Community And Deeper Relationships."

# I Just Need To Talk To A Real Person

**Text:** John 15:13-17

**Theme:** The Need For A Sense Of Community And Deeper Relationships

**Characters:**    Hattie, elderly lady
Heidi, Hattie's young niece
Voice over a microphone backstage

**Tone:** Humorous, empathetic

**Setting/Props:** Living room in Hattie's apartment, exaggerated large cell phone

**Approximate time:** 5-6 minutes

---

(Music, such as the piano playing of Lorrie Line, in an upbeat major key)

**Hattie:** *(Sitting in rocker and knitting)* I think I'll get myself something sweet. *(Gets up and goes to her cupboard)* Now let's see ... Where are my prunes? I love nibbling on prunes. *(Looks at audience)* And they are good for you, too. *(Chuckles)* But now, where are they? Oh my, I'm all out! Hmm, looks like I'm about out of food, period. Guess I need to call the grocery store. Let's see: some cereal, bananas, skim milk, bread, eggs, and, of course, some sweets like my "it'll keep you regular" prunes. *(Smiles at audience again)*
    Let's see; I need a refill on my pills, too. Only got two left. That'll just last me today and tomorrow.

This is a nice place my children had me move into. I'd rather be in my own house and neighborhood but "Mom," they said, "you've got to have it more convenient. You're not a spring chicken anymore." What am I, an old hen? *(Makes chicken sound)* So I moved into this apartment.

Let's see, where is that newfangled phone they got me? *(Picks up an exaggerated size cell phone)*

Kids said this cell phone would get me anything — anytime — anywhere I would ever need something.

I'd rather just go downtown like I used to. Sure miss my car. It was so nice to get out and visit with people. I get so tired of those talk shows, and the news is all bad ... Well, here goes — got to get groceries, medicine, a few supplies, and ... *(dials)*

**Recorded Male Voice Over Microphone:** Hello, shoppers. This is the Super Duper Store. Our hours are from 6 to 6. That's 24 hours for your shopping convenience. Super Duper Store offers free carts, abundant credit and today — canteloupes are on sale. Welcome, shoppers.

*(Hattie can spice up the following recorded message by her facial expressions as she is bewildered, amazed, surprised, disgusted, and a bit confused.)*

**Voice:** If you know the extension number you are trying to reach or if you know the last five digits of the store employee who will help you, enter that now.

If you would like to talk to the Meat Department and you have a push button phone, push 1 now. If you would like the Cereal Aisle, push 2 now. If you would like the Dairy/Freezer section, push 3 now. If you would like the Fruit Department, push 4 now. If you would like the Vegetable Table, push 5 now. If you would like the Cat and Dog Food Shelf, push the pound button and also push 6 now.

If you are a satisfied customer and desire the Pharmacy, push 7 now. If you want Hardware, push 8. When you get Hardware and you want either hammers or screwdrivers, push pound 8 now or the star key. If you want nails, screws ... *(Fade away momentarily in order to hear Hattie's comment)*

**Hattie:** *(Looks quizzically at receiver)* You've got to be kidding. Oh, my goodness!

**Voice:** If you do not have a push button phone, dial 0 now and an operator will help you. Thank you so much for your order. Your call is important to us.

**Hattie:** Well, maybe I can get some help now. *(Hattie exaggerates her frustration as she pushes button on phone)*

**Voice:** This is a recorded message from your Operator. All of our lines are busy right now so if you would like to leave a message, wait until after the beep. Remember, at the Super Duper Store your message is very important to us.

**Hattie:** Oh, mercy me! How am I going to get what I need? *(Puts cell phone down)* Kids left this pager for me to use. I can't remember how it works though. I need to talk to somebody. *(Moans softly)*
  Who can help me anyway? Social workers are busy. Home Health says I'm too healthy to qualify. Meals On Wheels delivers only meals. I know — I'll call 911 and groan and say, "I've fallen and I can't get up." Naw. I'd better not.
  *(Brightens up)* I know. I'll try my church. Why didn't I think of that before? *(Dials church)*

**Female Voice:** Hello. God bless you. This is St. Martin's Community Church. If you have a push button phone and you desire Holy Communion, push 1 now. If this is an emergency, dial 911. If you would like a Baptism, Marriage, or a Funeral, push 2 now. If you would like to speak to our Senior Pastor, push 3 now, or our Associate Pastor, push 4 now. If you would like our Youth and Education Director, push 5 now. If you would like the Devotion for the Day, push 6 now, and if you would like our Secretary, Malinda, please stay on the line and she or a recorded voice will answer your questions. Your call is very important to us. God bless you and thank you for calling St. Martin's Community Church.

**Hattie:** I can't believe it! My church has gone high tech, too. Oh, what's this world coming to? If I don't get my pills I won't be around long enough to find out.

Oh, I'm kinda tired. *(Lays down; lights dim; she prays)* O Lord, you came down as a person, didn't you? Where are all your people when I need 'em?

*(Knock-knock or door bell; Hattie wakes up)*

**Hattie:** Oh, oh, c-c-come right in. Oh, it's you, Heidi.

**Heidi:** Hi, Aunt Hattie. What's a favorite niece for but to visit her favorite aunt once in a while?

**Hattie:** Oh, Heidi, I'm so glad to see you. I haven't talked to anybody for three days.

**Heidi:** *(Looks at cell phone)* But what's that? I thought Mom got you that.

**Hattie:** Oh, yes, she did, bless her, but you know it just doesn't do what I need.

**Heidi:** What do you mean?

**Hattie:** I called the grocery store, the other day I called the post office, last Monday the doctor's office and would you believe just a little while ago I tried to call my church, and in every situation I got the same response. A mechanical voice answered me.

**Heidi:** Oh, I know how it is nowadays.

**Hattie:** Do you, Heidi? Do you?

**Heidi:** You are lonely, aren't you?

**Hattie:** *(Ignores Heidi's question; laughs)* If the disciples were living today, you know what would happen.

**Heidi:** *(Curious)* No, tell me, Aunt Hattie.

**Hattie:** If the disciples of Jesus had voice mail it would go like this: *(Hattie makes her voice sound like the recorded voices she heard earlier)* You have reached the office of Jesus of Nazareth. To confess your sins, press 1 now; to request a miracle, press 2 now; to hear a parable, press 3 now; to file a complaint, press 4 now; to schedule a baptism, press 5 now; to learn about the next sermon on the mount, press 6 now; to leave a message with one of the other disciples, press 7 now; and if you are using a rotary phone, give up. To repeat this frustrating process, push the pound button and scream now!

**Heidi:** *(Laughs heartily; Hattie joins her. They hug)* Oh, I love you, Aunt Hattie. Remember, you have me.

**Hattie:** And I love you, Sweetie.

**Heidi:** What you need, Auntie, is a cup of tea, and me and some good conversation. Tell you what — I'll do your errands for you —

**Hattie:** Oh! Wonderful!

**Heidi:** But I can't do 'em today — maybe next week — Bye, Auntie. *(Leaves)*

*(Hattie looks forlorn and dejected.)*

**Hattie:** *(Looks at cell phone)* Is this all I've got?

(Music in minor key)

The End

## No Longer Home Alone
John 15:13-17

*"No one has greater love than this, to lay down one's life for one's friends. You are my friends if you do what I command you. I do not call you servants any longer, because the servant does not know what the master is doing; but I have called you friends, because I have made known to you everything that I have heard from my Father. You did not choose me but I chose you. I appointed you to go and bear fruit, fruit that will last, so that the Father will give you whatever you ask him in my name. I am giving you these commands so that you may love one another."*

Friends in Christ,

Recently, we heard the news of a Chicago couple who left their two little girls **home alone** for nine days — unsupervised and uncared for. And the Chicago couple seemed surprised to be arrested upon their return from a vacation in Mexico. This story was a disturbing version of the hit movie *Home Alone*. We laughed at the box office hit, but the movie failed to portray the frightening side of it. It's not very fun to be left home alone, or isolated, ignored, or forgotten.[1]

Now we come to the second sermon in this series of six on the spiritual needs of Americans. Our focus is on George Gallup's discovery of this second need — **the need for a sense of community and deeper relationships**.

Dick Meyer tells about a woman who shared her story as a childhood polio victim. She said, "When my mother left me in Sunday School, I always asked her if I could wear her locket. She thought I liked it, but that wasn't it at all. I knew I wasn't worth coming back for, but I knew she would come back for her locket."[2]

Then there is the story of a woman who faked having cancer for two years. This woman cut off all her hair. She lost thirty pounds to make people believe she had cancer. She joined multiple cancer support groups. But she was found out when a health professional checked her story. She was so depressed when her boyfriend broke up with her, and she felt so alone, she decided to get sympathy and attention by pretending she had cancer.[3]

Mother Teresa once said, "The biggest disease today is not leprosy or cancer. It is the feeling of being uncared for, unwanted — of being deserted and alone!"[4] I believe she was right. The surveys show it and deep within our hearts we know it. Three persons in ten say they have been lonely for a long period of time.

A haunting song you still hear is "Eleanor Rigby." "Look at all the lonely people — where do they all come from?" Eleanor Rigby became the symbol of loneliness in the '60s and '70s, and we still hear it in the '80s and '90s and resonate to it. The Beatles were not singing the blues for themselves. They vocalized loneliness — the twentieth century's saddest disease — a condition brought on by the changes and strangeness of modern life.

There are concrete reasons for this epidemic of loneliness.

1. In 1940, most family members lived within 100 miles of each other and got together regularly for family times. They enjoyed uncles, aunts, grandparents and grandchildren sharing life together. Today, the average family consists of 1.5 parents and 1.7 children, with no blood relatives within 100 miles.

2. In 1940, the average person lived in the same neighborhood for a lifetime and got to know and care about the other people in the neighborhood like a family. Today, the average person moves every five years and the neighbors are often total strangers.

3. In 1940, the average person stayed with the same job for 25 years. Today, the average person changes jobs every seven years or is moved to another city to keep his present job.

4. In 1940, the neighborhood church was the center of the life of the average member — from the cradle to the grave.[5] Today, it is common to church shop every few years.

We've discovered as a people that to prevent the pain of saying good-bye, we no longer say hello.

So what George Gallup has discovered as a key spiritual need is this **NEED For A Sense Of Community And Deeper Relationships.**

The Bible teaches us three principles about loneliness and community and deeper relationships.

**1. We were created to belong.** When God created Adam, God said, "It is not good to be alone. I will make a helper suitable for him" (Genesis 2:18). One of the Scripture's first lessons is that by ourselves we are incomplete. We need others to fill the emptiness within us. We are created to be social, not independently self-sufficient. Robert Bellah's diagnosis of an out-of-balance individualism is highly accurate.

Ecclesiastes 4:9-10 says, "Two are better than one, because they have a good reward for their work. For if they fail, one will lift up the other; but woe to one who is alone and falls and does not have another to help."

C.S. Lewis said, "We are born helpless. As soon as we are fully conscious we discover loneliness. We need others physically, emotionally, intellectually; we need them to know anything, even ourselves" (*The Four Loves*, p. 12).

We were created to belong. It is not good to be alone. Jesus modeled such belonging behavior for us. He called the twelve to be **with** him. The New Testament Greek word is *koinonia*. It is more than fellowship — it is "life-sharing." That's why joining a church is one thing, but belonging to a church is another. When we belong we share life, we connect, we are a team, an empowered body.

Michael Jordan is considered the greatest basketball player that ever lived. Yet Michael Jordan never won a championship until the Chicago Bulls had the right players to support him.

God created us to belong to each other. Together we share our lives, resulting in deeper relationships.

**2. Jesus redeemed us for friendship.** I like the way Jesus defines "friendship" in our Gospel reading from John 15. He defines friendship as an event. "No one has greater love than this, to lay down one's life for one's friends" (v. 13). There is also the quality of taking one into one's confidence: "I have called you friend because I have made known to you everything that I have heard from my Father" (v. 15).

A friend will come through in a pinch: when you need help; when in crisis; when in trouble; when your car won't start; when your loved one dies; when you lose your job. Your friend comes through.

I was driving a borrowed pickup recently and six or seven miles south of Belle Plaine on Highway 169 I ran out of gas. It's a lonely feeling. But a young teenager who happened to be at home gave me some gas. I worried as I approached the farmhouse on foot that she would be afraid of me, so I quickly reassured her that I was a Lutheran pastor and she need not be afraid. She quickly slammed the door — (no, just kidding) — she cautiously welcomed me and became my benefactor and friend.

We know a friend by what he or she does for us. That makes friendship an event and not a feeling.

A friend is also determined by the degree to which one can take people into one's confidence. Is he or she trustworthy? Jesus said, "I have made known to you everything that I have heard from my Father."

Do you have one good friend? If you do, you are a most lucky person.

Three times, I remember, I was painfully lonely. The first time was when I was a child. I was literally home alone. I was not abandoned, but my parents just took a little longer to get home from town one night. Fourteen miles out in the country alone with a child's imagination running wild can be quite an experience. The second time was my second year at college. I was in a new state and a new college, with no friends, and loneliness gripped me and tried to smother me until my brother came along and got me reconnected. The third time, which still happens from time to time, is as a parish pastor. This business (ministry) can be awfully lonely, especially if you take public stands on unpopular issues.

Can you recall a time when you felt utterly and completely alone? Was it a move, a new job, a new school, or just life in general in these strange, detached times? And how did you feel when someone came to your side and walked with you?

Michael Guido writes in his column, "Seeds From The Sower":

> *My lawnmower had broken down and I had been working on it for hours, but all in vain. Just then a neighbor came along with a tool box.*
> *"May I help you?" he asked.*
> *"You may," I answered. And he fixed the mower in just a few minutes.*
> *"Thousands of thanks!" I exclaimed.*
> *"Oh," he answered, "you're welcome."*
> *Just as he was about to walk away, I asked, "What do you make with that beautiful set of tools?"*
> *"Mostly friends," he replied.*[6]

The Living Bible says, "A true friend is always loyal, and a brother is born to help in time of need."

Jesus said in John 15, "I no longer call you servants, I call you **friend**." Jesus redeemed us for friendship with him and for one another.

**3. Where in the world can we find this sense of community and deeper relationships?** Will the schools of higher education in our land provide it? Will the government or civic groups or sports teams or fraternities or sororities or guilds or book clubs or compact disk clubs? What or who has the capacity and power to bring Hattie some comfort?

We find a clue in Paul's letter to the Philippians. "I thank my God every time I remember you, constantly praying with joy in every one of my prayers for all of you, because of your sharing in the gospel from the first day until now" (Philippians 1:3-5).

If you and I cannot find health and healing — find acceptance and a sense of belonging, and affirmation — in the church of Jesus Christ, we will not find it anywhere. This is the greatest evangelistic time in history for the church of Christ. It is the greatest opportunity to bring people together as family — the family of God where love reigns, where sins are forgiven, and where we know we **belong**.

A letter came to the editor of a large city paper. It read, "I'm so lonely I could die, my phone never rings ... I'm the only one on earth. How else can I feel? All alone. See no one. Oh, dear God, help me ... will somebody call me?"

The letter containing $1 and six stamps for anybody who would call or write was signed, Jean Rosenstein. The *Los Angeles Times* printed the letter Thanksgiving morning, adding that Mrs. Rosenstein was an 84-year-old widow and retired nurse, living home alone in a tiny apartment on $200 per month.

The result was no less than a miracle. Jean Rosenstein received so many calls Thanksgiving Day she finally had to take the phone off the hook. "I hope people will forgive me," she told reporters on Friday, slightly hoarse. "I just couldn't talk anymore. The phone rang all night. I only got two hours of sleep."

The next morning, the letter carrier brought an armload of letters. Dozens of people stopped by her apartment. Many brought or sent flowers. Every table was covered with potted plants and the bathtub was full of flowers.

"I've got the most beautiful bathtub in the world," said Mrs. Rosenstein. To top it off she had to turn down many invitations and she had four turkeys in her refrigerator.[7]

You and I were created for others. We, by the grace of God, were created to belong. We were redeemed for friendship. We need to look no further for community. It's right here — in front of you and around you — before your very eyes. Amen.

---

1. *Faith at Work*, Volume 106, No. 1, Jan/Feb 1993, p. 2.

2. *Faith at Work*, Volume 106, No. 2, Spring 1993, p. 3.

3. *Ibid., FAW*, p. 3

4. *Ibid., FAW*, p. 3.

5. Lyman Coleman, *Training Manual for Small Group Leaders*, p. 5.

6. Michael Guido, Guido Evangelistic Association, used by permission.

7. Associated Press, 1970.

# 3

## *Worship Aid*

A Chancel Drama suggestion for the sermon, "You Are My Beloved," is titled "The Conference." It is an original drama by Arley K. Fadness.

**Synopsis:** A strangely behaving student and his parents have a conference with the school counselor about the student's behavior problems. Throughout the consultation, the student acts out strange antics in order to call attention to himself. The counselor shocks the parents with a surprising diagnosis and prescription at the end of the consultation.

This chancel drama is a setup for preaching to the theme of "The Need To Be Appreciated And Respected."

# The Conference

**Text:** Mark 1:10-11

**Theme:** The Need To Be Appreciated And Respected

**Characters:**   Dr. Hobbs, school counselor
Parents, Mr. and Mrs. Rosett
Dirk, troubled student

**Tone:** Humorous, underlying serious

**Setting/Props:** Counselor's office, chairs

**Approximate time:** 5-6 minutes

---

(School sounds may be heard, such as bells, announcements over a public address system, hall noise, etc.)

*(Troubled student and parents enter counselor's office)*

**Counselor:** C'mon in, Mr. and Mrs. Rosett — you too — ah er ...

**Parent 1:** ... ah, Dirk ...

**Counselor:** Come in, Dirk.

*(Dirk hops up on a chair with his feet on the seat, arms dangling like an ape, mouth open. He is obviously misbehaving and acts as though nothing is getting through.)*

**Counselor:** My name is Dr. Hobbs and I'm the school counselor here at _____ High School. *(Looks at paper)* I see you, Dirk, have been referred to me by Principal Burns, ah, and by, ah, four of your present teachers, the coach and, ah, by your pastor, Rev. Gullickson, and, ah, let's see, also by the local police department. Hmmmm. *(Reading)* "Behavior modification and temperament adjustment needed. There are symptoms of an underlying problem. Special attention is needed."

**Parents:** He *(points to Dirk)* doesn't **have** problems. He **is** a problem!

**Counselor:** And how do you feel about that?

**Parent 1:** He is disrespectful, uncontrollable, defiant, lazy, and ...

**Parent 2:** ... distant, aloof, ever since we cracked down on him.

**Counselor:** And when was that Mr. (Mrs.) Rosett?

**Parent 1:** Just last month when he started eleventh grade.

**Counselor:** *(Shocked)* You just gave him rules **last** month?

**Parent 1:** Yes, we pretty much let him make his own choices while he was growing up. After all, we both work — in fact, I have two part-time jobs to make ends meet.

**Parent 2:** Well, we both wouldn't have to work ... I am doing quite well ...

**Parent 1:** Nonsense. We need the money!

**Counselor:** Hmmm. Where are you at in all this, Dirk?

**Dirk:** *(Role plays an ape)* Ugh. Ugh. *(Points to fruit basket)* Ugh. Ugh.

**Counselor:** *(Role plays, too)* Okay, okay, Corky Dorky, you want a banana. I'll throw it into your cage. *(Tosses banana)*

*(Dirk sweeps it up, peels it, throws peeling into the audience, eats banana. Offers some to parents, who angrily reject it. Rubs stomach with a contented look.)*

**Counselor:** Hmmm — most unusual behavior. Acts like an ape, eh?

**Parent 1:** Dirk! Cut the crap! We've got serious business here.

**Parent 2:** *(To counselor)* Yesterday he was a kangaroo.

**Counselor:** *(Incredulously)* A kangaroo?

*(At the mention of "kangaroo" Dirk jumps down from his chair perch and begins to hop around like a kangaroo.)*

**Parent 1:** *(Groans)* We ignore him when he's like this. I suppose he wants something from us. We give him everything he needs.

**Counselor:** Maybe he's trying to get your ... ah ... attention.

**Parent 2:** Attention? We feed him. We buy him clothes. We send him on vacations. We gave him his own cell phone, TV in his room, boom box, CDs, swimming pool in our back yard — generous allowance, his new sports car ... What more can we give this parasite?

**Counselor:** *(Astonished)* Parasite? You call him a parasite?

**Dirk:** *(Breaks kangaroo stance; stands erect. Recites mechanically)* A parasite is a living thing that nourishes itself on another organism. A parasite is a beggar, cadger, sponger, scrounger, freeloader, leech, bloodsucker, loafer, slacker, shirker, deadbeat, goldbrick, moocher. *(Resumes kangaroo stance)*

**Counselor:** *(Shocked, to parents)* That's what you think of your son?

**Parent 2:** *(Sarcastically)* You notice, he does talk.

**Counselor:** Do you parents have regular conversations with your son?

**Parent 1:** Well, not really. We don't communicate except when we're shouting and breaking dishes. *(Scowls at Dirk)*

**Counselor:** Sounds kind of violent. Maybe Dirk is needing something **very** important.

*(Dirk nods yes as he drops his kangaroo stance.)*

**Parent 2:** Really important? What in blazes do you mean, counselor?

**Parent 1:** I don't have a clue as to what you're talking about.

*(Dirk assumes he is a clown by putting on a red nose and floppy hat.)*

**Counselor:** Now what is he?

**Parent 2:** Bozo the clown, I guess.

**Parent 1:** So it's attention, attention, attention he wants! We've only got so much to give.

*(Dirk acts out a brief scene in which he shows he wants love.)*

**Counselor:** Hmm. *(Pause)* I believe I have a solution. My diagnosis is this:

**Parents:** *(Eagerly)* Yes, yes.

**Counselor:** It is obvious at least to the trained mind that your son is neither an ape, nor a kangaroo, nor a parasite, nor a clown, but a **son** you have conceived and reared, rather poorly, I might add, but nevertheless, **your** son, who deserves your love and your attention. He is a human being made in God's image who needs and expects to be appreciated and respected as a person. I am writing a prescription for you, and it's really a family prescription that will affect you all. I am confident, with new health in your relationship, the problems which brought Dirk to my office will be abated and ultimately eliminated. *(Writes and gives sheets to parents)* See you in two weeks. My receptionist will make the appointment. Thank you, Mr. Clown. And thanks to you, Mr. and Mrs. Rosett.

**Parent 1:** *(Looks at sheet, aghast)* **I can't believe this!**

**Parent 2:** Believe what? *(Pleasantly)* Thank you, Dr. Hobbs.

*(Exit)*

**Parent 1:** *(Looks at prescription)* I can't believe this. This is going to **solve** Dirk's behavior problem?

**Parent 2:** Well, what does it say?

**Parent 1:** *(Reads)* "For your son, Dirk, to modify his behavior challenges, he will need to feel appreciated, respected, and loved. In order for this to happen, you three will spend one hour per day together in quality mutual pursuits, giving and receiving, working and playing in a reciprocal manner." Impossible!

**Parent 2:** Impossible? I think this is **not** impossible. In fact, this **is** possible. We are going to do it. *(Thinks for a few moments and then has an "aha" look. Reaches in Dirk's pocket and pulls out two red clown noses and puts one on. Then gives the second one to a reluctant Parent 1. They look at one another, laugh and begin to exit arm in arm.)*

*(Dirk nods excitedly. All exit)*

The End

## *You Are My Beloved*
### Mark 1:10-11

*"And just as He was coming up out of the water, He saw the heavens torn apart and the spirit descending like a dove on Him. And a voice came from heaven, 'You are my Son, the Beloved: with you I am well pleased.'"*

Brothers and Sisters in Christ,

I tell you a tale of a little village in an isolated land where the people shared a boundless sense of happiness. The people in this village showed only one unusual feature about their life together. They had a custom — a delightful custom — of **giving fuzzies** to each other. Something about fuzzies felt good and made people happy.

Then one day someone became upset over something petty and started a rumor of retaliation. "Have you heard about the shortage of fuzzies?" the disgruntled member of the community began asking.

Before long, the people began **hiding** their fuzzies. They buried them in fields, hid them in out-of-the-way places, and locked them in vaults. Only on birthdays and anniversaries did they wrap up fuzzies as special presents. In time they quit giving them altogether.

As you might expect, the little village developed into a miserable place to live. People became cranky and sad, gloomy and depressed. They began fighting, and strife broke out. Tension and suspicion replaced the former trust and good will.

Then one day, while some of the children were playing in a field, they stumbled onto a hidden cache of fuzzies. The tingle as they touched them felt wonderful. With delighted laughter they gave some to their friends. The more they gave away, the happier they felt. The adults soon noticed and remembered the good old days.

Soon they joined the fun and brought out their fuzzies from hiding. And, as you might expect, the village became a wonderful place to live again.

What are these fuzzies? Nothing more than honest compliments and true appreciation. Not flattery. Not kind words and deeds as a setup in order to manipulate — but true affirmations that build up another person's morale and self-esteem.[1]

I tell you this tale to introduce the topic for today.

This is a series of six sermons based on the six spiritual needs of Americans. The third need that George Gallup, Jr., identified in his survey is **the need to be appreciated and respected**.

George Gallup discovered that one-third of the American people have a **low sense of self-worth and self-esteem**. However, he also discovered that the closer people feel to God, the better they feel about themselves. An active faith can repair damage done by others.[2]

Susan Pickle, Human Development Specialist with the University of Missouri-Columbia Extension, discovered in her research these findings:

— Adults receive about 60 put-downs a day and most are given by themselves.

— 75 percent of adult thinking is negative.

— By age 4, the average child has had 25,000 put-downs.

— By fifth grade, only 20 percent of youth feel good about themselves.

— By high school graduation, only 5 percent feel good about themselves.[3]

It's like a great societal vacuum, a great black hole, a cosmic magnet that sucks away our good feelings and perceptions about ourselves, making us forget we are created in the image of God.

Marilee Zdenek has written a tender little book of poems titled *Splinters In My Pride*. She tells, "Once, I knew a little girl who spent her own money to buy a box of gold stars and stuck every one of them on a piece of paper that had her name on the top. I thought what an enormous need for a child to be loved — to buy enough stars so that the need for self-esteem is quenched."[4]

The text for this morning is a refreshing breeze. It's a text from Mark's gospel, chapter one, verses ten and eleven.

Let me take you back to the beginning of Jesus' public ministry. Let me take you back in time to the Jordan River, to Jesus' baptism. Look closely at what happened.

> *Just as Jesus was coming up out of the water, He saw the heavens torn apart and the Spirit descending like a dove on Him, and a Voice came from heaven, "You are my Son, the Beloved, with you I am well pleased."*

What an affirmation, especially at this point, as Dick Meyer points out, because Jesus has yet to do anything. He has not healed anyone. He has not preached a sermon. He hasn't told any parables or calmed any seas. And yet there is this affirming word from heaven: "With you I am well pleased. You are my beloved."[5]

What do these words tell us about God? What do they teach us about ourselves? Ten times you see these affirming words in the New Testament. And they remind us that God's acceptance has nothing to do with our performance. God loves us for who we are — not what we have **done**. Christ dies for us while we were yet sinners. Why? Because you and I matter to God. God speaks, not only to the Son, "You are my Beloved," but also to you and to me.

Henri Nouwen puts God's words this way:

> *I have called you by name, from the very beginning. You are mine and I am yours. You are my Beloved, on you my favor rests. I have molded you in the depths of the earth and knitted you together in your mother's womb. I have carved you in the palms of my hands and hidden you in the shadow of my embrace. I look at you with infinite tenderness and care for you with a care more intimate than that of a mother for her child ... you belong to me. I am your father, your mother, your brother, your sister, your lover, and your spouse ... nothing will ever separate us. We are one.*[6]

It is very hard to accept this "Beloved" stance — this "most favored position." One's immediate response is to **fight it**. We can **fight** it or **believe** it and/or **practice** it.

Coming out of our low self-esteem we naturally **fight** it.

I have a friend who, if you give her a warm fuzzie, a gold star, a true compliment, will fight it. I say, "I like your house." Her response is, "Oh, but the color is painted wrong; the steps are sagging; the hot water heater is going out," and she will discount and neutralize the compliment.

We do that. We recycle affirmations. Sometimes we are afraid that if we don't put ourselves down, someone else will, and that will be much more painful.

We need **to be appreciated and respected.** We need to hear, "You are my beloved," from God. You do matter to God. And we need it from one another. "You have worth in my eyes; you have value; you are gifted with gifts and potential; I like who you are; I admire you and I respect you and I appreciate you. I grow from you."

A letter to Dear Abby signed, "Spotted in Long Island," bemoaned the fact that a young lady saw herself practically ruined because she had freckles. Abby answered by suggesting she cover up her freckles if they bothered her. But the suggestion brought on a storm of responses, prompting this letter:

> *Dear Abby: Please tell "Spotted in Long Island" — the young woman with freckles — not to worry.*
>
> *I am a 68-year old woman with freckles and red hair, and I have felt her pain. I used buttermilk, stump-water, lemon juice, all kinds of bleaching creams and anything else that was suggested to make my freckles disappear. I still have freckles!*
>
> *When anyone dared to tell me I was pretty, I refused to believe him. I overheard someone say (about me), "She's beautiful, and the most beautiful part of it is that she doesn't believe it."*
>
> *Not until I was 60 years old did I realize that I had been pretty all my life. I meet people I haven't seen in 35 or 40 years, and they recognize me immediately and even*

*remember my name. Becoming gray hasn't changed me from "that redhead from Arkansas."*
*Our gift from God is who we are; our gift TO God is what we become. Make the most of what you have and be happy. Life is too short to be wasted. Sign me ... The Girl Who Swallowed A $20 Gold Piece and Broke Out in Pennies.*[7]

Eleanor Roosevelt said, "No one can make you feel inferior without your consent."

Rather than **fight** it — **believe** it.

God said in your baptism, "You are My Beloved." Brothers and Sisters who care say, "I think you're great"; "I think you're wonderful"; "I love you."

It won't be easy to believe it if you have had a lifetime of negativity and have been plagued with self-doubt and low self-esteem. But just think of where who you are starts. It starts in your baptism.

William Willimon says, "In Baptism we are initiated, crowned, chosen, embraced, washed, adopted, gifted, reborn, killed, and thereby redeemed. We are identified as one of God's own, then assigned our place and our job within the kingdom of God. The way for a Christian to find out who he or she is, is not to jump on the rear of a Honda and head west, but rather to come to the font and look into those graceful waters. The reflection of yourself which you see there is who you really are."[8]

Believe it. "You are my Beloved!"

I'll never forget the backward compliment I received from my father once. My boyhood neighbors and I had been rascals, playing jokes and pranks until one day we went too far ... Dad was furious with our behavior and he exploded and said to my friend, "This I would expect from you, but [looking at me] not from you." Then I realized the high expectations that Dad had about me. And over the years Dad communicated one way or another, "Arley, you're a great son. I value you. You're something!"

I was the Dean of my conference a few years ago. While helping a church secure a pastoral candidate, I asked, "What kind of a pastor do you want?" The call committee said, "We want a pastor just like Pastor Fadness." Obviously I was amazed and affirmed, and I never forgot the statement.

Don't **fight** it. **Believe** it. And then **practice** it, one to another. Say, "You are my beloved. You are my beloved friend. You are my beloved neighbor. You are my beloved son, daughter, spouse, significant other. You are my beloved employee, student, teacher."

And if you can't do it at first with **words** — begin with **deeds**. Acts of love and kindness have no bounds. They'll know — they'll know they are from one who is loved and changed by Christ.

Joan Benny remembers Sunday mornings as being her "special time" with her father, Jack Benny:

> *Daddy would wake me up for breakfast about 7:30. Then we'd head outside to go for a drive. Daddy would get into the car and turn the ignition key. Inevitably, nothing would happen. He would push and pull every button on the dashboard, twist all the knobs and pump the accelerator, but the motor still wouldn't start. At length he would sigh and say to me, "Honey, the car just won't start until you give me a kiss."*
>
> *So I did, and it did — and off we went. For a long time I believed there was some kind of scientific connection between kissing and car-starting.*[9]

The warm fuzzies are waiting. A thousand gold stars, too.

A kiss, a hug, a word, a deed — you are my beloved. I appreciate you. I respect you. Amen.

---

1. Story by Charles Mylander, source unknown.

2. *Faith at Work*, Volume 106, No. 3, p. 2.

3. Susan Pickle, Research at University of Missouri-Columbia Extension.

4. Marilee Zdenek, *Splinters In My Pride*.

5. *Faith at Work*, Volume 106, No. 3, p. 3.

6. *FAW*, Volume 106, No. 3, pp. 2, 10. From Henri Nouwen's *Life of the Beloved*.

7. As seen in a *Dear Abby* column by Abigail Van Buren. © Universal Press Syndicate, Reprinted by Permission. All rights reserved.

8. Quote from William Willimon used by permission.

9. Reprinted from *Sunday Nights at Seven: The Jack Benny Story* © 1991, Warner Books, New York.

# 4

## *Worship Aid*

A Chancel Drama suggestion for the sermon, "Is Anybody Listening?," is titled "Can Anybody Really Hear Me?" It is an original drama by Arley K. Fadness.

**Synopsis:** Mary Delight is a young lady representing Generation X who is bewildered about her future. Mary goes to trusted individuals for a caring ear but is not listened to and gets frustrated. Finally she blurts out her dilemma to a little child, and the child seems to hear and care.

This chancel drama is a setup for preaching to the theme of "The Need To Be Listened To And Heard."

# Can Anybody Really Hear Me?

**Text:** Luke 8:8b

**Theme:** The Need To Be Listened To And Heard

**Characters:**   Narrator
　　　　　　　　Mary Delight
　　　　　　　　Pastor Lovet, wearing clerical collar
　　　　　　　　Sam, Mary's employer at the Deli, wearing apron
　　　　　　　　Mr. Harpie, band teacher
　　　　　　　　Scooter, little child

**Tone:** Thoughtful, humorous

**Setting/Props:** All characters on stage are frozen until spoken to. When each character finishes his dialogue with Mary, he or she then resumes the frozen position.

**Approximate time:** 5-6 minutes

---

**Narrator:** Once upon a time there was this young lady, Mary Delight, who came to that juncture in her road of life when she wondered, "Should she, Mary Delight, marry Harry, or should she seek knowledge and go to college, or might she at nineteen pierce her ears and work for Sears?"

Mary was in that common quandary so many who are called Generation X find themselves in. You know what a quandary is? A quandary is a puzzling predicament requiring a decision and a focus. Let's ponder with Mary Delight and see how it is going.

**Mary D:** *(Dressed in a brightly flowered outfit, Mary sings, hums, whistles a happy, carefree song. She appears on stage with high energy, doing cartwheels, or rollerblading, or some youthful, active action. She picks a flower and gives it to a person in the audience, flits here and there, and then suddenly sits down and becomes pensive, and ponders)* It's been a blast. Cool. That's for sure. *(Thoughtfully)* But now I'm in a real bind. Tomorrow is my twentieth birthday — **I'm getting old!** *(Laughs)* Not really old old. *(Seriously)* But I do need to make up my mind.

Should I marry Harry? He says he loves me and I love him, too, but ...

Or should I get some more knowledge and go to college? Folks want me to. They said they'd help me anyway they could. Dollars for scholars.

Or should I take that job at Sears? You know it would be interesting. Oh, what shall I do? *(Wrings her hands, twirls her curls)*

I know, I'll talk to our new pastor — The Rev. Dr. Emmet J. Lovet. *(To Pastor Lovet)* Hi, Pastor Lovet.

**Pastor Lovet:** Hello, Mary.

**Mary D:** Pastor, I know you haven't been at our parish very long, but I do have a personal question to ask you ...

**Pastor Lovet:** Personal?

**Mary D:** *(Laughs)* Personal about **me**, not you!

**Pastor Lovet:** Oh. Go ahead.

**Mary D:** I'll be twenty tomorrow.

**Pastor Lovet:** So?

**Mary D:** *(Set back by his abrupt, insensitive demeanor)* Well, I must make some decisions for my future.

**Pastor Lovet:** Fine. Go on. I'm listening. *(Reads a book)*

**Mary D:** What I mean is, should I marry Harry, or go to college and get some knowledge, or pierce my ears and work for Sears?

**Pastor Lovet:** *(In stained-glass voice, insensitively)* That's a real dilemma, Mary. When I was your age I already knew what I planned to do. Why, when I was twelve years old, I managed the neighborhood paper route, went on to college, majored in English and Hebrew, all the while working, working my way through college, and then seminary ... And furthermore ...

**Mary D:** ... but I feel ...

**Pastor Lovet:** No matter what you feel, Miss Mary, here's what I think ... The Bible says ... *(Pastor Lovet freezes)*

**Mary D:** *(Turns away, disappointed)* No help there. Wish Pastor Truett was around. He seemed to know exactly how I felt and never "preached" at me. Maybe I'll talk to my old boss at the Deli.

**Sam:** Hi, Mary. *(Jokingly)* You're late or very, very early for work. *(Laughs)*

**Mary D:** Hi, Sam. *(Laughs)* No, I'm just stopping by to say "Hi" and ...

**Sam:** Good to see you, Mary. *(Continues to work at baking a pastry)*

**Mary D:** ... and I just need to talk to someone who will listen to me.

**Sam:** *(Interrupts)* Thanks for staying over the noon hour yesterday. We sure were rushed and with Nancy gone and all.

**Mary D:** Oh, no problem. *(Pause)*

**Sam:** You're the best.

**Mary D:** Why, thank you. *(Pause)* I've been wanting to talk ...

**Sam:** *(Interrupts)* I've had three quit on me this year.

**Mary D:** Oh ... ah ... I'm sorry to hear that ... ah, Mr. Sam, I've been struggling with ...

**Sam:** I'm planning on setting up a new department.

**Mary D:** Oh ...

**Sam:** Pharmaceuticals — customers need drugs. They'd really like that convenience. Can't help but improve business. I could even give my clerks a raise. *(Laughs)*

**Mary D:** Oh, that'd be great. Ah, Sam, I really ...

**Sam:** Store across the street is my fiercest competitor ... and ... where are you going, Mary?

**Mary D:** *(Mary turns to leave)* I need to go. Thanks for listening. *(Rolls her eyes sarcastically)*

**Sam:** Bye. Wonder what she wanted. Little unusual to stop by like that on her day off. *(Sam freezes)*

*(Mary sees her old teacher)*

**Mary D:** Mr. Harpie!

**Harpie:** Hi, Mary Delight. Long time ...

**Mary D:** no see. *(Laughs)*

**Harpie:** Been out two years now?

**Mary D:** Yep. And I do *miss* the band.

**Harpie:** That was a great year. Your clarinet solo was awesome.

**Mary D:** You really thought so?

**Harpie:** Sure — I've got eighteen clarinets this year. We're going to Chicago and then New Orleans for the National Band Festival. Want to chaperone?

**Mary D:** Wow, that's great. No, I don't think so. *(Pause)* Ah, Mr. Harpie, I was wondering ...

**Harpie:** Get your way paid.

**Mary D:** Oh? *(Blurts out)* I'm trying to decide to decide, do I marry Harry, or go to college and get some knowledge, or pierce my ears and work for Sears?

**Harpie:** *(Obviously not listening)* Be gone two weeks. We've got a superb repertoire. All of Sousa's greats. Carl Orff's works, and some fun pops stuff.

**Mary D:** I don't think ...

**Harpie:** I can just see the Towerville High School Band performing and me directing. *(Directs; becomes oblivious to Mary, then freezes)*

**Mary D:** *(Disillusioned)* Oh, what am I going to do? *(Wrings her hands, then shouts)* **Can anybody listen for a minute? Hear me out?**

**Scooter:** Hi, Mary.

**Mary D:** Oh, hi, Scooter. What do you want?

**Scooter:** Nuttin'

**Mary D:** Well ... *(Waits for Scooter to talk)*

**Scooter:** I miss talking to you, Mary.

**Mary D:** Oh, I miss talking to ... really?

**Scooter:** Yep, you're my pal.

**Mary D:** And I'm your friend. Say ... ah ... I've got a problem. *(Waits to see if she gets interrupted)*

**Scooter:** I'm all ears.

**Mary D:** *(Looks around in bewilderment; smiles and sits down)* Okay, Scooter — I have been wondering, tomorrow is my birthday and I've been thinking ... *(conversation fades away as concluding music is brought up)*

The End

# Is Anybody Listening?
## Luke 8:8b

*"As Jesus said this, he called out, 'Let anyone with ears to hear listen!' "*

Brothers and Sisters in Christ,
 A mother and her small daughter were discussing the dolls in a department store. "What does it do?" the child would ask about each one. The mother would answer as each doll was examined, "It talks," or "It wets," or "It cries." The dolls were rather expensive, so the mother tried to direct her little girl's interest toward a plainer doll that was more reasonably priced. "How about this one?" "Does it do anything?" the child asked. "Yes," the mother replied. "It listens." And the little girl quickly and eagerly reached for the doll.[1]
 The Gallup poll, which we are using thematically in this sermon series, identifies **the need to be listened to, to be heard and understood** as the fourth important spiritual need of modern Americans.
 In prior sermons I have dealt with our need for meaning and purpose, our need for a sense of community and deeper relationships, and the need to be appreciated and respected. Now the topic is the need to be **listened to and to be heard**.
 I attended a synod planning meeting recently in Owatonna. It was a task-focused meeting. We gave reports, we made plans, we made decisions, and we left. And as we walked out to our cars in the parking lot, I turned to Bob, the organist from Albert Lea, and I said, "How's it going for you?" He looked at me and said, "My father-in-law died this week. No warning — suddenly died — in his late fifties." And it struck me like a blow to the head how nine of us came together for this meeting — we worked, did our tasks, and went home, and never took time to listen to the real issues of

our personal lives. So I took a few minutes out there in that parking lot and listened to Bob's loss and sadness.

In our congregation we are teaching L L D D — Love, Learn, Do, and Decide — as the staple format for our gatherings. We let the first "L" stand not only for **Love** but also for **Listen**.

Paul Tillich said the first duty of love is to listen. And psychologists say that deep listening is indistinguishable from love.

Our need **to be listened to** is critical. Ever feel like you're talking to a wall? Sometimes your spouse seems like a wall. Or your child is a wall. Your employee is a wall.

We can sympathize with the little boy who needed a minor operation. His ward in the hospital had an intercom system which enabled the floor nurse to talk to her patients. That night, however, her efforts to reach the boy were in vain. "Timmy," she said into the intercom, "I know you're there. Why don't you answer me?" There was a long pause. Then a small, quavering voice asked, "What do you want, Wall?"[2]

One day I walked into a department store in the Mall Of America in the cities and I casually turned to this lady and said, "It's an amazing store, isn't it?" No response. Thought I was talking to a wall. But I wasn't. I was talking to a mannequin. Embarrassing.

Perceptive doctors report that frequently they will see patients who really have nothing physically wrong with them. They merely need someone to listen to them.

I know of a bartender who claims that although customers are billed for their drinks, they are really paying for someone to listen to them. "Lonely people don't come to a bar just to drink," he says. "They can drink at home and a lot cheaper. They come in to my bar to find someone who will listen to them and usually I'm it."[3]

Jesus says in our Gospel reading this morning, seven simple words: "Let anyone with ears to hear — listen."

Have we lost our ears? On *Prime Time* recently they carried the sad story of children born with no eyes. It's a rare disease. What a tragedy to go through life with no eyes. But I wondered about a greater tragedy: Are we becoming a generation of children and adults with no **ears**? We neither listen nor are listened to. And when we're not heard, we feel unimportant and discounted.

"Let any one with ears to hear — listen." I need to be listened to and heard. Hear my dreams, my frustrations, my joys, my troubles.

You and I can be encouraged this morning to know in the first place that **God listens**. God is not earless.

In Psalm 66:16-19, it is clear:

> *Come and hear, all you who fear God, and I will tell what he has done for me. I cried aloud to him, and he was extolled with my tongue. If I had cherished iniquity in my heart, the Lord would not have listened. But truly God has listened; he has given heed to the words of my prayer.*

God listens.

And I love that passage in Ezekiel 3:12-15 where the prophet-priest Ezekiel came to the people of Israel in exile by the river Chebar and said, in essence, "I sat where they sat." I lived with them. I felt with them. I wept with them. I sat where they sat. This is a picture of God, a preview of God coming at Christmas in the incarnation of Jesus. God came to sit where we sit, to feel what we feel, to weep when we weep.

A little girl sobbed, "Mother, Susie dropped her doll and broke it."

"Did you help her fix it?" her mother asked.

"No," said the girl. "But I helped her cry."[4]

God listens.

We are most blessed when we have a friend, counselor, pastor, or confidante who listens. How lucky to have a friend who listens deeper than the words to feelings and aspirations and the wildest dreams — what a friend! It's pure bliss to be listened to.

I have a cousin who listens to me. I know he's interested. He draws me out. He says, "Tell me more." He asks questions; he probes. He listens. He makes me feel worthwhile. I feel like I am somebody.

The late Dr. Karl Menninger wrote about the effects of being listened to in his book *Love Against Hate*: "When we are listened to it creates us, makes us unfold and expand ... it makes people happy and free when they are listened to."

As Christians we are called to the ministry of listening. We are called to listen in two directions: to God and to others.

First, we listen to God. Luke 19:47-48 says, "Every day Jesus taught in the temple ... all the people kept listening to him, not wanting to miss a single word."

A golden opportunity to listen to God is at worship. That's why we put such a high priority on worship around here. That's why we emphasize celebrative traditional and contemporary worship. It is at worship that we listen to God with our ears and our hearts.

A man lost his watch in a pile of sawdust. Workers went through it with rakes, but could not find it. When they left for lunch, a little boy went to the pile and came out a little later with the watch.

"How did you find it?" they asked.

"I just laid down and listened," he answered.[5]

When you and I lose something — happiness, peace of mind, a sense of forgiveness — we need to wait on God and listen for the ticking in the sawdust.

We are called, in the second place, to listen to **others.** "Bye, whoever is listening," my son Tim said one morning on his way to school.

Martin Luther insisted that every Christian is a priest. Luther listed among the priestly functions of the laity: to pray for each other, to listen to their sisters' and brothers' confessions of sin and cries of distress, and to speak God's cheering word of forgiveness and consolation.

We are called to listen to each other.

But how is this done? Luke 8:18a says, "Then pay attention to **how** you listen ..." We listen well when we take the word E A R S as our guide.

Let **E** stand for **eye.** We listen best with our eyes. Eye contact is unbeatable. The eye lock is a powerful magnet for connecting with people.

I have a friend who, when she talks to me, is always on the hunt with her eyes for someone more important or more interesting to enter the room. She's distracted. But when one's eyes say, "You are the most important person in my presence at this moment," it's dynamite. We listen best with concentrated, connected eyes.

Let **A**, the second letter in the word EARS, stand for **affection**. I listen best when I communicate love for the speaker. My love moves me to empathy, which is "to feel with someone." When I sit where he sits, when I feel what she feels, I listen well. When I say to myself, "God loves this person and I love him/her, too," it makes a big difference. I listen best with affection.

Let **R** stand for **reliable**. Good listeners never break confidence. They are trustworthy. They zip the lip.

An inebriated man came stumbling out of a bar and almost knocked down his minister, who happened to be walking past.

"Oh, Pastor, I'm so sorry for you to see me like this," he said.

"Well, I don't know why you should be sorry for me to see you this way, Sam. After all, the Lord sees you now, doesn't he?"

"Yeah," said the drunk, "but he's not such a blabbermouth as you are."

Good listeners keep confidence. They are reliable.

Let **S** stand for **sparing with advice**. People seek not curing, as Dick Meyer says in his book *One Anothering,* but caring. It is more blessed to care than to cure. The good listener is sparing with advice.

The world is to be listened to and heard. The world needs EARS.

**Listen to the Children**
*Take a moment to listen today*
*To what your children are trying to say.*
*Listen today, whatever you do,*
*Or they won't be there to listen to you.*

*Listen to their problems, listen to their needs.*
*Praise their smallest triumphs, praise their smallest deeds.*
*Tolerate their chatter, amplify their laughter;*
*Find out what's the matter, find out what they're after.*

*But tell them that you love them,*
*every single night,*
*And though you scold them, make sure you hold them,*
*And tell them everything's all right.*

*Take a moment to listen today
To what your children are trying to say.
Listen today, whatever you do,
And they will come back to listen to you.*[6]

Amen.

---

1. Source unknown.

2. *Faith at Work*, Volume 106, No. 4, Fall 1993, p. 3.

3. William Diehl, "Our Ministry of Listening" from *Faith In Action*, p. 14.

4. Michael Guido, Guido Evangelistic Association, "Seeds From the Sower."

5. *Ibid.*

6. Source unknown.

# 5

## Worship Aid

A Chancel Drama suggestion for the sermon, "Growing In God's Freedom," is titled "Same Old, Same Old." It is an original drama by Arley K. Fadness.

**Synopsis:** A husband and wife argue about how to celebrate their 23rd wedding anniversary. Alma, the wife, likes to go to the same romantic place where they went on their honeymoon, year after year. George, the husband, is tired of the "same old thing" and would rather go or do new things. The debate is seemingly unresolved until Alma is seen looking at a brochure titled "Tahiti" and is heard making a call to a travel agency. This abrupt change indicates a sudden growth spurt in their relationship.

This chancel drama is a setup for preaching to the theme of "The Need To Feel That One Is Growing In Faith."

# Same Old, Same Old

**Text:** John 8:31-36

**Theme:** The Need To Feel That One Is Growing In Faith

**Characters:** Alma, wife, wearing an old, outdated wig
George, husband, wearing an old, outdated sweater

**Tone:** Humorous

**Setting/Props:** Home setting, telephone, large travel map

**Approximate time:** 5-8 minutes

---

**Alma:** Say, George.

**George:** Say, what?

**Alma:** I think it's time.

**George:** Time for what, dear?

**Alma:** You know.

**George:** I know?

**Alma:** Yes, Sweetie — it's time ...

**George and Alma:** ... to plan our anniversary.

**George:** *(Protests)* But that's three months from now.

**Alma:** That's exactly the point.

**George:** Point?

**Alma:** We haven't much time.

**George:** *(Groans)* Three months **needed** for planning our 23rd wedding anniversary and we do the same old thing again and again?

**Alma:** *(Feigned shock)* Why, Georgie — how dare you talk disrespectful of our sacred time together.

**George:** That ain't it.

**Alma:** Well, what is it?

**George:** To always go to the North Shore on our anniversary just because ...

**Alma:** *(Finishes his sentence)* ... just because that was where we spent our honeymoon. I thought you were in heaven on our honeymoon, staying in that quaint cottage by the old lighthouse and all — water lapping on the shore while we walked in the sand hand in hand.

**George:** *(Stutters)* W-well, yes, but ...

**Alma:** ... but it's always the same old thing. I know, I know.

*(Phone rings. Alma answers, talking ad lib to her friend Yappy about how she and George are planning to plan their wedding anniversary. George rolls his eyes and performs various antics during her conversation, implying that all this "anniversary talk" is getting goofy.)*

**Alma:** That was Yappy, George. I told her about our plans. Okay. Let's eat. Supper's ready and we'll finish our discussion, eh? *(Ties bib on George, sets food in front of him, starts to feed him)*

**George:** Alma! I'm not an invalid. I can feed myself. I'm ...

**Alma:** I'm a grown man ... I know, Georgie Porgie ... I know. *(Continues to fuss over him)*

**George:** My arm has healed, you know.

**Alma:** How long has it been since you broke it?

**George:** Two years ago last September and you **still** treat me like a cripple or something ... I just ...

**Alma:** I just will do it myself. I know, I know. *(Eats in silence)*

**George:** Now you're mad?

**Alma:** Nope! *(Really angry, but can't admit it)*

**George:** About our anniversary ...

**Alma:** Forget it!

**George:** Okay — we'll forget it.

**Alma:** *(Changes her tune)* No, no. *(Condescendingly)* I'll adjust.

**George:** *(Tries to make up)* North Shore's fine. September 5th.

**Alma:** *(Warms up)* Oooh, it'll be soooo romantic — you and I — just like 23 years ago. Gooseberry Falls, a walk along the shore, skipping stones in the lake, watching the freighters, the sea gulls, climbing Artist's Look Out, sketching a sunset ...

**George:** Twenty-three years? *(Rolls eyes. Telephone rings. George answers.)* H'lo. George. George Blankly, Oh, it's you, Tom. Fine. How are you? Trip? With you and Gladys? Bill and Mary? Fishing, eh?

**Alma:** *(Looking concerned)* When, George, when?

**George:** First weekend of September? That'll be great. Let's do it. Thanks, Tom. Bye. *(Hangs up receiver; excitedly)* It's all planned!

**Alma:** *(Skeptically)* What's planned?

**George:** A fishing trip to Montrose in Canada. We're going with the Karnes and the Stoffens.

**Alma:** Did you consult me?

**George:** You love fishing.

**Alma:** I know, but did you **consult** me?

**George:** I know, but it's easier to ask for forgiveness than permission sometimes.

**Alma:** Permission isn't the issue. What's the date, George?

**George:** Let's see — first weekend in October — ah, no. First weekend in September.

**Alma: First weekend in September!??? George, have you lost your marbles?**

**George:** *(Stunned)* Oh! That's right!

**George and Alma:** Our anniversary trip to North Shore.

**George:** Okay, okay, I'll call them back *(Alma glares; George talks on phone in low tones while Alma makes dingbat signs while looking at the audience and pointing to George)*

**Alma:** Can you believe that? A fishing trip on **our most** sacred weekend?

**George:** All settled. We'll go fishing later in the fall. Now what planning do we need to do?

**Alma:** Oh, George, if you're going to be so glum about this ...

**George:** Forget it! Maybe we should! Same old, same old ...

**Alma:** No, no. *(Pause)* By the way, how long have you worn that same old, same old sweater? And sat in that same old, same old chair? And smoked that same old, same old corn cob pipe?

**George:** What do you mean? What are you getting at?

**Alma:** How long, George? Answer me.

**George:** *(Meekly)* Twenty-three years or so.

**Alma:** Aha! Same old, same old.

**George:** *(Defiantly)* How long have **you** been wearing that mop — er — wig? *(Exits)*

**Alma:** *(Sits for a while and thinks; jumps up)* That's it! *(Looks in mirror; adjusts wig; takes new wig out of box; looks in mirror)* You know, maybe George is right. *(Picks up large brochure titled "Tahiti," reads it, picks up phone, and dials travel agency. George reappears with a new bright sweater and new pipe but is not seen by Alma.)* Hello, Nelson's Travel Agency? Could you give me some information on a trip for two to Tahiti?

(South Sea island music plays in the background.)

The End

## *Growing In God's Freedom*
John 8:31-36

*"So if the Son makes you free, you will be free indeed."*

Brothers and Sisters in Christ,
After worship, a little boy told the pastor: "When I grow up, I'm going to give you some money." "Well, thank you," the pastor replied, "but why?" "Because my daddy says you're one of the poorest preachers we've ever had."[1]

With the risk of this story in mind, I am pleased, nevertheless, to bring you the fifth sermon in a series of six, dealing with the spiritual needs of Americans as discovered by George Gallup, Jr.

This morning, we focus on **the need to feel that one is growing in faith**. I begin with a song by Peter Pan.

> *I won't grow up.*
> *Not a penny will I pinch.*
> *I will never grow a mustache*
> *or a fraction of an inch.*
> *'Cause growing up is awfuller*
> *than all the awful things that ever were.*
> *I will never grow up, never grow up,*
> *never grow up, not me!*[2]

So sang Peter Pan ... and for some of us it is our song. We don't want to grow up. We do not want to face the next stage in life. We are comfortable where we are. In fact, we don't know why anyone would want us to change. Like Peter Pan, we express our desire to stay just as we are.

There was a group of Peter Pans in the New Testament. Listen to how the author of the Letter to the Hebrews feels about growing up in Christ, or more accurately, the **lack** of growing up in faith.

*For though by this time you ought to be teachers, you need someone to teach you again the basic elements of the oracles of God. You need milk, not solid food; for everyone who lives on milk, being still an infant, is unskilled in the word of righteousness. But solid food is for the mature, for those whose faculties have been trained by practice to distinguish good from evil.*
— Hebrews 5:12-14

The Peter Pans in the Letter to the Hebrews did not want to grow up. Here is an example of frozen spiritual development. Here are people who have been professing Christ for years. By this time they ought to be teachers. They've had plenty of time, says the writer to the Hebrews, since believing in Christ, to be able to instruct others about the basics of the Gospel message — but they never left their babyhood.

I have seen 20-, 30-, 40-, 50-year-old people who are still lying in their baby cribs. I have been there myself — stuck — sitting in kindergarten — a grown man, sucking on a baby bottle. We keep taking classes in Christianity 101.

And yet according to George Gallup, Jr., there are thousands of us who actually do want to grow up. We have the urgent need to feel that we are growing in our faith. I know I want to grow in my faith and life. I want to grow intellectually, emotionally, and spiritually. I do want to mature and learn and expand my faith. Ignorance is not bliss. Immaturity is not attractive. Peter Pan may think it's wonderful, but Wendy and her brothers, after spending time in Never-Never Land, discover differently.[3]

On this beautiful Lord's Day, we celebrate knowing three things: We celebrate knowing we are **free**. We celebrate knowing we are **free to grow**. And thirdly, we worship God knowing we are free **to grow up**.

**We rejoice knowing we are free.**

We read in John's gospel, "If you continue in my word, you are truly my disciples, and you will know the truth and the truth will make you free ... so if the Son makes you free, you will be free indeed."

The Reformation proclaimed three major principles: justification by grace through faith, the authority of the Scriptures, and the universal priesthood of the baptized. This morning we are overwhelmed by the truth of the first — that by God's grace in Jesus Christ we are forgiven, cleansed, healed, made perfect and sinless. We are justified — made right with God — through the cross of Christ and him crucified. God's Son has made me free.

There is that story told about Abraham Lincoln. "Lincoln went down to the slave block. He saw a young girl being sold. He took money out of his own pocket and bought her. When she was brought to him, he said, 'Young lady, you are free.' She said, 'Please, sir, what does that mean?' He said, 'It means you are free.' 'Does that mean,' she asked, 'that I can say whatever I want to say?' Lincoln said, 'Yes, my dear, you can say whatever you want to say.' 'Does that mean,' she asked, 'that I can be whatever I want to be?' Lincoln said, 'Yes, you can be whatever you want to be.' She asked, 'Does that mean I can go wherever I want to go?' He said, 'Yes, you can go whenever you want to go.' And the girl, with tears streaming down her face, said, 'Then I will go with you.' "[4]

When the Son makes you free, you are free indeed.

We can rejoice in the second place, knowing and feeling **we are free to grow**. We are either trees or posts. You can take a tree and put it in the ground, and it begins to grow. When you put a post in the ground, it begins to rot and decay. We are trees or we are posts. As a pastor these years, it has been my delight to see people in my congregation grow like trees. Unfortunately, I have also had to witness the sad business of watching posts decay and fade away. Are you a tree or a post?

John Westerhoff, Christian Education Specialist, writes in his thesis cassette series titled *The Development of Faith* that faith has content and can change its characteristics through life. Some faith developmental theorists see the Christian believer going through various stages and levels of maturity in life. Westerhoff pictures the analogy of a tree. "A one-ring tree is a whole tree; has all its treehood, no less than a three-ring tree and the same is true of faith. A tree grow one ring at a time — gradually — so it is with faith." Depends on environment, on nourishment.

I want to be a tree. I want to celebrate that God's Son has made me free to grow. I expect to grow ring by ring.

Thirdly, we can rejoice this morning knowing we are free **to grow up**. I'll never forget my two boy cousins, brothers who were very nasty to each other. I remember as kids one brother shouted to the other, on a Sunday afternoon when we were visiting, "Shut up!" Now "shut up" was never allowed nor said in the home I grew up in. It was close to profanity. Then my ears were shocked to hear Charles retort back, "I don't shut up, I grow up, and when I look at you, I throw up!"

God calls us to maturity in our newfound freedom. Wouldn't it be a joke, if this morning we announced a potluck for the parish but the only food we could bring, share, and eat, would be Gerber's baby food? The time for milk is over. We are free to grow up!

James Taylor says we are like naked crabs.

> *When you go to the seashore, every pool and puddle left by the retreating tide seems to have a crab in it. I've seen them. Little ones scuttle sideways, squeezing under rocks, peeking out from a patch of seaweed, occasionally venturing out to nibble on some unsuspecting human toe. Now and then you may see bigger crabs, in deeper, safer pools. With great majesty they wave their huge claws as a warning to stay clear.*
>
> *On the beach, shells of crabs lie washed up by the waves. Some are from crabs that died. Others are simply discarded, a dwelling too small for its growing occupant. That's how crabs grow bigger — when their shells get too tight, they split the shell open and grow a new one.*[5]

I've never talked to a crab. But I imagine the process of splitting open a shell must be painful. I'm sure that until they grow a new shell, they feel terribly defenseless and vulnerable. They're literally naked. That's how we feel when we crack open our shells.

Our shells aren't visible, like the crab's. But they are there, just the same, shells formed by years of habit, shells that protect us from other people, shells that are the roles we play as parents or children or bosses or employees. Every now and then, we crack our shells open and emerge into a new world, quivering and defenseless. Teenagers do it as they become adults. No wonder, James Taylor says, they get crabby. I did it in the '60s when I had to think new thoughts about race relations and war. Adults do it as they learn to quit running their children's lives. Or when they lose their jobs, or divorce strikes, or a spouse dies, or one's home burns up, or when an investment fails.

But we are free to grow up and bear fruit by the grace of God.

I remember Norman. He and his wife were in our Twelves group in a past parish. This particular group consisted of Lutheran and Roman Catholic mixed couples. They met together in homes, discussed the faith — both similarities and differences — and prayed together. One night Norman said, "I always prayed for the conversion of my Lutheran wife (to Roman Catholicism) and now I pray a different prayer — a prayer for growth and deeper understanding in the common faith."

God never leaves us as God finds us.

I am changing, by the grace of God and by the movement of the Holy Spirit. God is maturing me. I am not today what I was yesterday, nor what I'll be tomorrow.

So I will celebrate. I am free. God's Son has made me free, free to grow, free to grow up in Christ. Amen.

---

1. "The Joyful Noiseletter," Volume 8, No. 9, November, 1993.

2. *Faith at Work*, Volume 104, No. 1, Jan/Feb 1991, p. 3.

3. *FAW*, Volume 104, No. 1, Jan/Feb 1991, p. 3.

4. Source unknown.

5. Parable by James Taylor titled "Naked Crabs."

# 6

## *Worship Aid*

A Chancel Drama suggestion for the sermon, "Surrounded By Help," is titled "The Dilemma." It is an original drama by Arley K. Fadness.

**Synopsis:** Mime appears on the stage and receives a note instructing him (or her) to do a specific task. The mime is terribly frustrated because he has no tools or guides. Then little by little further "helps," such as blueprints, tools, and specifications arrive. Soon the task can be accomplished. Everyone celebrates.

This chancel drama is a setup for preaching to the theme of "The Need For Practical Help In Developing A Mature Faith." An intentional and clear tie-in must be made in the sermon so that the wordless actions are completely understood.

# The Dilemma
# (A Pantomime)

**Text:** Ephesians 4:11-16

**Theme:** The Need For Practical Help In Developing A Mature Faith

**Characters:** Person with white face (like Marcel Marceau) in black tights
Stagehand
Pastor
Construction worker
Carpenter's assistant
Plant in audience
Other actors, as desired

**Tone:** Magical, light

**Setting/Props:** Circus music, large notes, blueprints, tools

**Approximate time:** 5-8 minutes

---

(Live or taped circus music introduces the scene.)

Mime appears on stage in black tights, turtleneck, socks, and white gloves. Bows, greets audience wordlessly, makes imaginary small talk with various people, and does busy things.

Stagehand appears carrying a large note at least 3' by 3' with instructions readable by the audience which says, *"Please build a box for the fox."*

Mime looks at a pile of boards (previously pre-cut for simple assembly into a box for the fox), scratches head, and ponders for a long time.

Mime looks at the pile from every angle. Gets very frustrated. Conveys the fact that he/she does not know how to build a box for the fox. Pretends to get advice from anyone nearby. Writes advice down, but the advice is of no use. Tears up notes.

Stagehand brings in another note which reads, *"Build box for fox now."*

Mime gets more frustrated, confused, and upset. Acts out antics reflecting growing stress and anxiety over the assignment.

Stagehand appears again with a note in larger red letters, saying, *"Build it now!!!"*

Mime reacts in different ways:

1. Looks at note — acts out helplessness. Gives up. Withdraws. Occupies him/herself with a ball or knitting, and so forth. Takes a nap. During nap other actors may appear, look at the notes, look puzzled, and then disappear.

### And/Or

2. Looks at note — motions for a "plant in the audience" to build it. No response. Mime is disappointed.

Finally, as the music changes to a brighter, livelier sound, a Pastor in clerics comes along with a set of blueprints and shows the Mime how to build the box for the fox.

Next a Construction Worker appears, bringing with him a construction hat, and explains safety measures.

Next an Assistant Carpenter brings a saw.

The Mime saws a board.

Mime finds a hammer, and so forth, and soon is able to build the box for the fox.

When the project is assembled, a sign is put up which reads, "A box for a fox." The box may be for an actual fox (use a picture) or a person named Mr. Fox. The Mime is joyful and celebrates with dancing and happy antics. The music selection can accent the actions with careful choreography (a suggestion: Handel's "Hallelujah Chorus").

The End

## *Surrounded By Help*
Ephesians 4:11-16

> *The gifts he gave were that some would be apostles, some prophets, some evangelists, some pastors and teachers, to equip the saints for the work of ministry, for building up the body of Christ, until all of us come to the unity of the faith and of the knowledge of the Son of God, to maturity, to the measure of the full stature of Christ.*

Brothers and Sisters in Christ,

I have a story I love repeating. "On Lake Michigan there is a cooling water outlet from a power operation station. Over the last few years, many swimmers have drowned in the unexpected deep trough carved by the fast, flowing waters near the outlet.

"Now there is a family, obviously an extraordinary family, who lives on the bluff overlooking the power station outlet. Some years ago now, this family assessed the dangerous situation and made a decision. They went out and bought a large Newfoundland dog. These dogs, the Newfoundlands, are bred to save people — people in trouble, swimming in threatening waters. And this family, clearly gifted with an uncanny insight and a sense of humor, named their new dog 'HELP.' "

And now you know, as Paul Harvey would say, "the rest of the story."

"When some hapless swimmer has gotten caught in the swirling, whirling waters, he instinctively cries for 'HELP' and this enormous brown dog leaps to his aid."[1]

This morning we conclude our series on the six spiritual needs of Americans as discovered by George Gallup, Jr., in his comprehensive survey — with the sixth spiritual need being **the need for practical help in developing a mature faith.**

In this series, we have considered the need for meaning and purpose in life, the need for a sense of community and deeper relationships, the need to be respected and appreciated, the need to be listened to and heard, and the need to feel that one is growing in faith. Finally, we consider the **need for practical help in developing a mature faith.**

In 1988, as the ELCA (Evangelical Lutheran Church in America) was being formed, representatives from the ELCA's Division for Congregational Life joined with five Protestant denominations to help shape a major study on the elements of effective Christian education. This study was conducted by the Search Institute in Minneapolis and funded by the Lilly Foundation and the participating denominations.

Eight marks of faith were examined. And the results from 110 ELCA congregations and 2,400 participants showed with an **integrated** faith or an **undeveloped** faith. Twenty-four percent of adults in this survey displayed an integrated or developed faith, whereas almost half showed an undeveloped faith.

By any survey, by any measurement anybody wants to devise and use, it is clear we American Christians need Help! I need Help. You need Help. We all need Help in developing a mature faith.

A member of his congregation told Rev. Warren J. Keating, pastor of First Presbyterian Church, Yuma, Arizona, that this was the best prayer he had ever heard. "Dear God, please help me be the person my dog thinks I am."[2]

The Good News in the Search survey is that most Lutherans **want** to grow in faith. "Over two thirds report that they want to: a) develop a more personal relationship with Jesus; b) learn more about the Bible; c) learn how to apply faith to daily living; d) improve skills in caring, loving concern for others; e) learn how to be a good spouse or parent; f) discover how to make moral decisions."[3]

More good news is that Help is on the way. Let me explain. Let us audit our resources. When you think of the saints of the church, both living and dead, not only their memory, but their influence and their example — the saints model the mature Christian life. And they become for us, under the influence of the Holy Spirit, a powerful force in helping us mature in the faith.

Paul writes to the saints in the Ephesian church about **special** saints called **gifts**. The **gifts** that God has given were apostles, prophets, evangelists, shepherds, and teachers (Ephesians 4:11). Paul is aware of the need of the Ephesian church to **grow up**. Today I want to focus on the last two gifts on the gift list: namely, shepherds and teachers. The Greek for *shepherd* is translated *pastor*, and some translators marry pastor to teacher so you have Pastor/Teacher in one.

What is the task of the shepherd/teacher/pastor? Paul explains, "To equip the saints for the work of ministry, for building up the Body of Christ" (v. 12).

Let me tell you that your shepherd/pastors are not overworked. In fact, we are underemployed. Our calling, as your pastors, is **to equip the saints (all the baptized believers) for the work of ministry, in order to build up the Body of Christ**. We are to preach, teach, and lead. True, we get exhausted and feel overworked when **we** do the work of ministry. But our calling is to equip **you** to do the work of ministry.

And it's good to remember who you are. You are the saints — the baptized believers. And it's good to remember that glorious picture of the saints painted by the writer to the Hebrews: "Therefore, since we are surrounded by so great a cloud of witnesses, let us lay aside every weight and run ..." (Hebrews 12). And how often have we sung, "Will the circle be unbroken, by and by, Lord, by and by?" Can you see the circle of the saints, past, present, and future, in the stands, cheering us on — shouting, "Run, run! Don't give up! Keep up the fight"? And here on earth, you have the shepherd/pastor/teacher to equip you and to train you by preaching, teaching, and leading.

And why? What is the purpose of all this?

So that "all of us come to unity of the faith and of the knowledge of the Son of God, to maturity, to the measure of the full stature of Christ ... we grow up in every way into Him who is the Head" (Ephesians 4:13, 15).

While on vacation in Wyoming, I saw a bumper sticker which read, "I Will Not Grow Up." And I laughed at this young whippersnapper, driving his 4x4 with a gun rack in the back window and his truck box full of adult toys. We feel that way sometimes. We also feel like that other bumper sticker which reads, "Honk if your horn is broken." We do need help.

Paul said, "We must no longer be children, tossed to and fro ... by every wind of doctrine, by people's trickery, by their craftiness in deceitful scheming" (Ephesians 4:14). We must grow up. We shall grow up!

I hear three cries for Help this morning: **Help me read and understand the Bible; help me pray;** and **help me in a closer walk with Christ.**

In the first place, **help me read and understand the Bible.** Help me get into the Scriptures and benefit by them. For it is the task of Shepherds to lead, guide, feed, and nourish the flock.

"The chief channels of grace," writes Lowell Erdahl in *Authentic Living*, "are scripture, sacrament, prayer, groups, and service."[4] "Help me read and understand the Bible." The good book is good for us. We wisely ponder at least one passage a day, marking vital insights and applying them to our lives. "The B-I-B-L-E, that's the book for me," our children sing.

In the book, *Children's Letters to God*, one letter read:

> *Dear God,*
> *Your book has a lot of zip to it. I like science fiction stories. You had very good ideas and I would like to know where you found them.*
> *Your reader — Jimmy*[5]

"Lutherans will **fight** for the Bible, will **die** for the Bible, but won't **read** it," says Harry Wendt of Crossroads. But Help is on the way — your Shepherd(s) is (are) here. And the place for you and me is in intentional Bible Study under the guidance and leadership of your pastors. "Help me read, understand, and apply the Bible to my life."

The second cry is **"Help me pray."** "God answers prayer in four ways," says Jess Moody. "Yes, no, later, and you've got to be kidding!"

Madeleine L'Engle, poet/writer, said in an interview in *The Other Side* magazine, "Prayer is like playing the piano or writing poetry. You don't do it well every single day, but unless you do it every single day, you're never going to do it well at all."[6]

The ship was sinking fast. The captain called out, "Anyone here know how to pray?"

One man stepped forward: "I do, captain."

"Good," said the captain. "You pray. The rest of us will put on life preservers. We're one short."

"Lord, help me pray." Help is on the way — help is already here.

Prayer vigils, prayer retreats, prayer services, prayer resources galore, help in praying out loud, help in praying conversational prayer, help in praying in the tradition of the Eastern Church as well as of the Western Church. Prayers that are public; prayers that are personal. Prayers that are spoken and prayers that are sung. Prayers whispered and prayers shot like arrows heavenward.

You and I are surrounded with helpers who know why we pray and how to pray.

Ann Landers received this letter about prayer:

> *"Dear Ann: A friend invited our family to her home to dinner. At the last moment her stove went on the bum and she called to say we would have to eat out. She and her husband and their three children met our tribe at a neighborhood restaurant.*
>
> *When the food arrived, my friend tapped her glass with the spoon and announced, "Please bow your heads for grace." I thought it was a nice gesture, but my husband was visibly upset. On the way home, he told me he thought grace in a public place was improper if not sacrilegious. I might add that he was brought up in a family where grace was never said, they just dived in — like hogs. Comment, please. — Wilma"*
>
> *Ann replies: "If grace is a part of the family custom, I see nothing improper or sacrilegious about saying it in public. If praying was the worst thing people did in public, this would be a beautiful world."*[8]

The Benedictine monks reversed the saying, "prayer is work," to "work is prayer." They saw everything they did as prayer.

When we see prayer as being as natural as breathing, permeating our thoughts, actions, and entire life, then we are growing up to the measure of the full stature of Christ.

Thirdly, **Help me into a closer walk with Christ**.

We get closer to Christ as we get closer to one another, like the spokes of a wheel get closer, the closer they get to the hub. Christ is our hub. The saints are spokes. Their grace and their love surround us; consequently, we feel the very presence of Christ.

I want to end with a word about Esther. Esther died, not too long ago. She was and is a saint of God. Esther was a gift giver in life. And she was a gift giver in her death. One of the last gifts she gave when she died was a prayer vigil, designed by her family, at her memorial worship. People came, received a votive candle, lit it, and were gently instructed to pray before the worship. Many came, were pleasantly surprised by the invitation, bowed and prayed, and were blessed. Thank you, Esther.

And that's what the saints do. They help us. They gift us as they surround us with God's love. And they cheer us on to grow up in Christ. Amen.

---

1. Story from *The Other Side* magazine, 300 West Apsely St., Philadelphia, PA 19144. Used by permission.

2. *Joyful Noiseletter* by the Fellowship of Merry Christians, P.O. Box 895, Portage, MI 49081-0895.

3. *Effective Christian Education Search Institute Study* by the Search Institute, Minneapolis, MN.

4. Lowell Erdahl, *Authentic Living*, copyright by Abingdon, p. 85.

5. Eric Marshall, *Children's Letters to God*, copyright 1966, Simon and Schuster, Inc., New York, NY.

6. Madeleine L'Engle, interviewed in *The Other Side* magazine, 1977. Used by permission.

7. *Joyful Noiseletter*, FMC.

8. Ann Landers' column, CRA, Chicago *Tribune*, 435 N. Michigan Ave., Chicago, IL 60611. Permission granted by Ann Landers and Creators Syndicate.